Setting
People
Free

COURSE WORKBOOK

Setting People Free

COURSE WORKBOOK

DAVID DEVENISH

KINGSWAY PUBLICATIONS
EASTBOURNE

First published 2001

Unless otherwise indicated, biblical quotations are from
the New International Version © 1973, 1978, 1984
by the International Bible Society.

ISBN 1 84291 011 6

Published by
KINGSWAY PUBLICATIONS
Lottbridge Drove, Eastbourne, BN23 6NT, England.
Email: books@kingsway.co.uk

Designed and produced for the publishers by
Bookprint Creative Services, P.O. Box 827, BN21 3YJ, England.
Printed in Great Britain.

Setting People Free

COURSE SYLLABUS

SEMINAR 1: **Foundations for Biblical Counselling**

- Aims of this course   1
- Biblical foundation for the counselling and caring ministry   1
- A biblical view of mankind   3
- Use of spiritual gifts   4
- Particular gifts helpful in counselling   4
- How do we move more in these gifts?   6

SEMINAR 2: **Essential Foundations of Salvation**
           and Baptism in the Holy Spirit

- Faith   7
- Repentance   8
- Baptism in water   9
- Baptism in the Holy Spirit   9

SEMINAR 3: **Caring Skills**

- The importance of listening   11
- Recognising defence mechanisms   11
- Balancing counselling and prayer ministry 12
- The power of words   12
- Understanding body language   13
- Empathy   14
- Bringing correction   14
- Confidentiality   15
- Avoid cross-sex counselling   15

SEMINAR 4: Physical Healing

- Growing faith   16
- Healing is to be seen as functioning within an atmosphere of loving care   16
- Getting to know the roots of an illness   17
- Faith   17
- The prayer time   18
- Persistence   20
- Different ways in which God heals/answers prayer   20
- What about those who are not healed?   20

SEMINAR 5: Overcoming the Effects of Past Hurts

- Understanding emotions   23
- Common emotional bondages   24
- How do we lead a hurt person to open up?   27
- Once the person has begun to open up   27
- Methodology: values and principles   28

SEMINAR 6: Healing the Demonised

- Biblical background   31
- How do people become demonised?   33
- Symptoms of demonisation   33
- Preparation for ministry   34
- The deliverance procedure   35
- Aftercare   37
- Backlash   37

SEMINAR 7: Practical Implementation

- Prayer ministry during and after services   38
- Ministry teams   39
- Dangers in this ministry   39
- The cost of this ministry   42

Appendix   43

Foundations for Biblical Counselling

1 Aims of this course

● To give a foundation for the ministry of setting people free, which is based on:

  a) the application of biblical truth to people's lives

  b) the expectation of the Holy Spirit moving in power

  c) the use of caring skills which are consistent with the biblical revelation of the character of God

  d) the belief that 'counselling' must not be separated from 'discipling' and therefore needs to take place primarily within the context of a local church

● For local churches to become equipped with people who are trained and open to God.

● To be a small part of seeing the whole church of God restored to being a place for the healing of the nations.

We recognise that many Christians do not live in freedom. Furthermore, as we see people converted from backgrounds of major emotional damage, we need to find biblical ways of helping them.

2 Biblical foundation for the counselling and caring ministry

a) We are to continue and express the ministry of Jesus

Jesus is described as the 'Wonderful Counsellor' (Isaiah 9:6). Note that this title is used in the context of the extension of God's rule.

Jesus came to proclaim freedom for the prisoners and to release the oppressed (Luke 4:18). He saw the crowds as 'harassed and helpless' (Matthew 9:36).

b) Two biblical words are used to describe the counselling ministry

- *Parakaleo*, meaning to encourage or beseech, literally to draw alongside (Hebrews 3:13).

- *Noutheteo*, meaning to admonish or change behaviour.

Our objective is to bring about changes in people's:

- behaviour
- attitudes
- motives

We are all to serve in this way, but counselling or encouraging is a particular ministry that some people have (see Romans 12:8).

Note 2 Corinthians 1:4.

c) We are to love one another (John 13:34)
Counselling should be a caring expression of our love to each other, not a professional/client relationship.

d) We are to carry each other's burdens (Galatians 6:2)
This is the law of Christ and should be the attitude of His people.

e) We are to assume personal responsibility for our lives

- This is never to be undermined. In Galatians 6:5 'load' (denoting a soldier's kit) is a different word to 'burden' (v 2).

- The aim of all counselling is to help people accept responsibility (see Ezekiel 18:2).

f) Teaching is important
Jesus had compassion on the crowds so what did He do? 'He began teaching them many things' (Mark 6:34). He responded to their need to receive truth because 'the truth will set you free' (John 8:32).

3 A biblical view of mankind

a) Evaluation of some secular psychological theories

i)   Behaviourist

ii) Freud

iii) Non-directive counselling

iv) Transactional analysis

b) Mankind is the peak of God's creation, created in the image of God

This is described in Genesis 1–2. Note that:

- both male and female are created in God's image

- emphasis is on man in fellowship and community

- mankind is endued with creativity and with choice and responsibility

- all people have value, but a value derived from God

c) Mankind is a unity (1 Thessalonians 5:23)

d) Mankind has fallen (Genesis 3)

The effect of the Fall was:

- guilty fear

- acute self-consciousness

- bias towards wrongdoing

- arrogant independence

The rebellion expressed in the Fall affects every part of human life in broken relationships with God, with others, with nature and within ourselves.

e) The image of God is not completely destroyed and our derived intrinsic value remains (Genesis 9:5–6)

f) Mankind is restorable in Christ

- We are being transformed into the likeness of God (2 Corinthians 3:18).

- There is no difference between male and female (Galatians 3:28).

- Our relationship with God has been restored through the cross. This means that our relationships with each other, within ourselves (peace of God) and eventually with nature are also being restored.

- Our value is re-emphasised in Christ.

When counselling, always consider others better than yourself (see Philippians 2:3).

4 Use of spiritual gifts

We expect God to move in power as we pray with a person needing help. The moving of the Spirit brings an 'economy' to our counselling, but does not mean we ignore legitimate caring skills. Spiritual gifts can be manifested through the one being prayed for as well.

5 Particular gifts helpful in counselling

a) The gift of tongues

This can be used:

- to build ourselves up

- to open us to the presence of God

- to bring brief petitions to God when we are not sure what to do next

- as a sign

b) Interpretation of tongues

This is a supernatural revelation through the Holy Spirit which enables the believer to communicate in the listener's language, the 'dynamic equivalent' of a tongue. It can come in a counselling time as well as in a public meeting.

c) Prophecy

This is the ability given by God to receive from Him and communicate an immediate message of God to others. It can be in words, in pictures and in actions.

d) Discernment of spirits

The supernatural gift of perception given by God to enable us to distinguish the motivating spirit behind certain words or deeds. The origin can be human (e.g. someone's own hurt spirit communicating), divine or demonic.

e) Words of wisdom

This is the special ability to receive from God insight on how a particular situation is to be resolved.

f) Word of knowledge

The supernatural revelation of facts about a person or situation which are not learned through the efforts of the natural mind but are fragments of knowledge, freely given by God, disclosing the truth which the Spirit wishes to be made known concerning a particular person or situation.

g) Gift of faith

A supernatural surge of confidence from the Holy Spirit, giving a certainty and assurance that God is about to act.

h) Miracles and gifts of healing

6 How do we move more in these gifts?

a) By being open to the Holy Spirit and having our minds less full
    of all our own ideas, doubts, frustrations, tensions, etc. It is
    good to pray 'Come, Holy Spirit' to experience the manifest
    presence of God. The Holy Spirit dynamic is essential in
    Christian counselling.

b) Through worship and prayer (Matthew 7:11; Luke 11:13).

c) By learning in a team context.

Essential Foundations of Salvation and Baptism in the Holy Spirit

1 Introduction

- As counsellors we must be ready to lead people to Christ and see that godly foundations are established.

- Many Christians' problems are due to the fact that when they came to Christ, they did not understand fully what was required of them and what God had done. Foundations are important.

- We need to have a clear understanding of the gospel, so we can give a brief summary to those seeking help, for example:

Jesus was born into the world as a man, lived a perfect life, died on a cross to carry the guilt of all our wrongdoing, rose again from death and now lives for ever. We need to repent of our wrong, believe in the truth about what God did on the cross and follow Jesus as our Lord, willing to obey Him in everything. We need to be baptised in water and receive the power of His Spirit to live a new life. We shall be saved from eternal punishment and be given eternal life.

2 Foundation of faith

a) Believe that God exists (Hebrews 11:6); that Jesus died on the cross to save sinners and that He rose again (Romans 10:9).

b) Faith is a matter not only of believing facts but of believing in a person (Romans 10:10).

   The heart implies accepting the lordship of Christ (see Mark 10:17–29).

c) Faith is verbal. Encourage people to pray their own prayer and tell others what God has done for them.

d) Faith will result in works (Acts 6:7). Be careful about announcing publicly that someone has 'become a Christian' before you have seen their 'works of faith' (James 2:14–26).

3 Foundation of repentance

This has often been underplayed and has sometimes resulted in Christians being troubled by sins from their past, long after their conversion.

a) Repentance should be specific.

b) Repentance involves accepting responsibility for one's own sin, not making excuses such as:

> 'It's the way I was brought up. I didn't have a father, you see.'

> 'Anyone as depressed as I was ...'

> 'I had been hurt so much.'

c) Repentance involves renunciation. The Oxford Dictionary defines 'renounce' as 'to abandon, surrender, give up, decline association with, withdraw from, discontinue'.

d) Repentance should be audible, especially when sins have been habitual, obsessional or occultic.

e) Repentance should be visible: 'Produce fruit in keeping with repentance' (Luke 3:7). This will involve:

● apologising and working to restore damaged relationships

● restitution of stolen goods

● getting rid of objects that lead to temptation (Acts 19:19) or provide reminders of past life

f) There is a significant difference between repentance and regret.

4 Foundation of baptism in water

- Linked with starting the Christian life (Acts 2:38, 41; 10:47; 22:14–16).

- Part of making disciples (Matthew 28:19–20).

- Explained as part of the gospel (Acts 8:36).

- Involves a grave, which signifies the end of the old life and the beginning of the new (Romans 6:3–5).

- Should be as soon as they have come to Christ and shown proof that they have repented (Acts 10:48; 16:33; 26:20).

5 Foundation of baptism in the Holy Spirit

a) What is baptism in the Holy Spirit?

i) It is the experience available to every Christian of receiving the power of the Holy Spirit and thus being enabled to use spiritual gifts, experience the assurance of God's love, and be effective in witnessing to Jesus and serving Him in the body of Christ, the church.

ii) A dynamic filling of the Holy Spirit:
- pour out (Acts 10:45)
- anoint (Acts 10:38)
- drink (John 7:37)
- come upon (Acts 1:8)
- fill (Ephesians 5:18)

iii) It is not the same as 'being touched' by the Holy Spirit.

iv) It is separate from conversion, though it may happen at the same time or subsequently.

v) It is clear that it has happened. There is usually audible evidence:
- speaking in tongues (Acts 2:4; 10:46; 19:6)
- prophecy (Acts 19:6)
- an overflow of praise (Acts 10:46; Romans 8:15)
- boldness in witness (Acts 1:8)

b) The importance of baptism in the Holy Spirit

i) Jesus taught His disciples (Acts 1:4–5).

ii) It is available to all believers (Acts 12:17–18, 39).

iii) It is an important foundation when missing (Acts 8:14–17; 19:1–6).

iv) Christians often seek help with problems when they have not experienced this fresh power necessary for living the Christian life. Biblical counsel will no doubt be helpful, but without the foundational experience of baptism in the Holy Spirit, people are being robbed of the power God has made available to them for overcoming the issues they may be facing. They also need to be encouraged to go on being filled continually with the Holy Spirit (Ephesians 5:18) and not regard their baptism in the Holy Spirit as a one-off event which recedes into the past and loses its freshness and effectiveness over time.

c) How to pray for people to be baptised in the Holy Spirit

i) Ensure the person is convinced biblically.

ii) Encourage them into a position of faith.

iii) Clear up reservations and obstacles such as:
- sin
- emotional issues

iv) Explain that you will lay hands upon them (Acts 8:12; 19:6).

v) Expect them to experience some of the gifts of the Holy Spirit.

Caring Skills

1 The importance of listening

a) As Christian carers we must learn to listen on two levels:
   - to what the person being counselled is saying
   - to the Holy Spirit

b) Do not be quick to advise (James 1:19).

c) Good listening involves being more aware of the other person than yourself.

d) Focus on the feelings that lie buried beneath the words.

e) Reflect back to the person the content and emotions contained in what they have said.

f) Be non-judgemental. Do not express your horror!

2 Recognising defence mechanisms

Common defence mechanisms:

a) compensation/sublimation

b) displacement

c) projection

d) introjection

e) rationalisation

f) denial

g) fantasy

h) regression

i) idealisation

j) reaction formation

k) deflection

l) 'conversion'

m) withdrawal

n) isolation

3 Balancing counselling and prayer ministry

There are two dangers to be aware of.

- Sometimes we can counsel, listen and advise extensively, without ever coming to the point of inviting the Holy Spirit in.

- We can be too quick to start praying when we need to listen to the person (and to God).

4 The power of words

a) We can speak words of encouragement or discouragement. How do people feel when we have spoken to them? (See James 3:1–12.)

b) Avoid trite and insensitive phrases, such as:
    - 'You need to have more faith, don't you?'
    - 'Praise the Lord anyway!'
    - 'We all have days like that.'
    - 'That happens to us all.'

c) Avoid responding by immediately talking about your own experience.

d) Avoid coming up immediately with a solution.

e) Use words of knowledge sensitively (see John 4:16).

f) Avoid acting on words of knowledge without confirmatory remembered evidence.

5 Understanding body language

There are three aspects of communication. Studies estimate that our words carry 7% of our message, while our tone of voice carries 38% and our non-verbal body language 55%.

The condition of our own spirit also communicates, e.g. anxiety, pushiness, anger, concern, love, etc.

a) Cultivating good body language

i)   Focus directly on the person with whom you are talking.

ii) Don't get too close – respect people's 'personal space'.

iii) Use proper eye contact.

iv) Match your facial expressions to what the person is telling you.

b) Observe the body language of the person

It can express:

i)   cutting off

ii) insecurity

iii) fear

iv) closing off – an unwillingness to express emotions

c) Encourage an open body attitude in the person you are praying with

d) The effects of 'spiritual' activity

The following manifestations may be evident:

i)   falling

ii) shaking

iii) screaming

iv) weeping

v)   laughter

vi) Other possible physical effects:
- 'drunkenness' (Acts 2:15; Ephesians 5:18)
- twitching
- eyelids fluttering abnormally
- hot spots
- heat
- hands quivering, tingling

However, there are not always such effects. We must seek God, not particular dramatic effects, and the important thing is fruit in changed lives.

6 Empathy

Empathy literally means 'feeling into' someone else's situation and problem.

a) Be aware of the other person's feelings on a moment-by-moment basis.

b) Sometimes empathy is a supernatural God-given ability and operates as a word of knowledge or gift of discernment of spirits. In this sense sometimes it involves interceding for the person (feeling on their behalf) even if they are still 'closed off' to it.

7 Bringing correction

a) Challenge sin.

b) Sin can cause people to 'lose' their healing (John 5:1–5).

c) Sin can also open a way for demons to come back (Luke 11:24–26).

d) We need to confront sin when praying with people. 'I'm willing to pray for you that root causes be dealt with, if you are willing to let go of your sin.'

e) We are not being kind to approve a Christian continuing in sin, even though we are to accept them as a person.

8 Confidentiality

a) Confidentiality is absolutely essential. Avoid such things as 'I'm just sharing this for prayer' or 'Don't tell anyone else but...'.

b) 'Confidentiality' can be used as a weapon of manipulation. This can end up putting the counsellor in the difficult position of not being able to do anything about a problem.

c) Within the context of a local church a better notion for counselling than confidentiality is 'stewardship of counsel'. 'I will not share your confidences with anybody who is not part of the problem or part of the solution', e.g. the person who has done the hurting may have to be spoken to, or those overseeing the counselling may need to know in order to help bring about the solution. Explain the 'stewardship of counsel' concept before you start to help people.

d) Total confidentiality is not always a safe or legal option. There are situations where outside authorities, e.g. church leaders or social services, must be informed.

9 Avoid cross-sex counselling

A fundamental value in Christian counselling is that we do not counsel or become involved in prayer ministry unless someone is present of the same sex as the person being counselled.

Physical Healing

1 Introduction

We need to remember that God heals in different ways. Do not become in bondage to:

a) any particular method of healing;

b) whether healing is instantaneous or a process over time.

2 Growing faith

It is true that in the Western world we do have a battle for faith in relation to physical healing. We are battling against the stronghold of the Western worldview. For this reason, we need to meditate on God's word concerning healing and continue to pray and step out in faith based on God's word.

Two key scriptures:

a) John 14:12–14. Note the context is that of miracles.

b) James 5:13–16. Seems to describe an expectation of normal church life.

3 Healing is to be seen as functioning within an atmosphere of loving care

- God gives particular ministries of healing.

- The person ministered to must know you love them whatever the immediate prayer outcome.

- Ongoing prayer is also important. We care for the sick as well as praying for their healing, including practical care.

4 Getting to know the roots of an illness

Man is a unity; our minds, emotions, spirits and bodies are interconnected. Hence sickness can have different roots.

- Sin (e.g. John 5:14). Sins in emotional areas, such as bitterness, are important in this connection. See also James 5:15–16, 'Confess your sins'.

- Emotional difficulties: fear, insecurity, perfectionism, tension and stress.

- Demonic (Acts 10:38).

- Curses on an individual or a family.

- Excessive pressure of work.

- Overtiredness.

- Heredity factors.

- Functional discord (i.e. purely physical).

How we pray can be determined by our discernment of the root. Also if sin, pressure of work or overtiredness is the genuine root cause, we need to take specific action.

5 Faith

a) Faith is often referred to in the Bible in the context of healing. 'Faith is the medium through which God releases His healing power' (John Wimber).

b) Faith is almost always present when a healing takes place, but can be operating in various people involved, for example:
    - The sick person (Acts 14:8).
    - Friends or relatives of the sick person (Luke 5:20; 8:41). On the other hand, relatives or close friends present when praying can be a hindrance because of an overly emotionally charged atmosphere.
    - The person praying (James 5:15).

- General faith in a church or meeting in response to teaching or a word of knowledge.
- Faith is often simply the determination to step out.

6 The prayer time

a) Public prayer times

Currently, what I usually do is:

i)   Call people forward for specific conditions which I believe God has laid on my heart.

ii) Personally pray for each of these individuals. There needs to be a balance between a belief in 'every member' ministry and a recognition of the anointing on the speaker or leader.

iii) Call people to come forward (or stand up) if they want prayer for healing for conditions not named, then proceed as above, usually with ministry team also initiating prayer.

iv) Have an openness to words of knowledge, although note that this is not an opportunity for long counselling.

v)   Speak to the sickness. This is not the time for long intercession. Encourage people to do what they could not do before.

b) Small, ministry-team situations

i)   Ask the question 'What is wrong?' This does not mean a full medical analysis. To those untrained in medicine this can be confusing and can hinder faith.

ii) We listen on two levels:
   - Natural. Evaluate what they are saying in the light of biblical knowledge and experience.
   - Supernatural. Be open to God for words of knowledge, etc.

iii) Examine why the person may have such a condition. It may not be what they think, e.g. they may trace a bad back to a physical accident, when the cause may be emotional or demonic.

People can suffer because of pronouncements by authority figures, e.g. self-fulfilling prophecies. If a doctor is convinced that a person won't get better, sometimes their well-intentioned words may become an obstacle to faith for healing.

iv) Various types of prayer are appropriate in different situations:
- a surge of faith for a specific healing prayer
- intercession – standing before God for that person
- encouraging the person to pray for their own healing
- prayer for emotional circumstances surrounding the problem if relevant
- words from God, e.g. a word of command in a burst of faith
- rebuking an evil spirit

This is not the place for long wordy prayers, trying to 'persuade' God to heal, but rather praying the words given us by God.

v) Continue to ask questions:
- 'How are we doing?'
- 'Is it feeling better?'
- 'Is anything going on?'
- 'Is it worse?'

vi) Give advice on what they should do to keep their healing or what to do if they are not healed.

NB The laying-on of hands to the hurting part is often not appropriate when praying with a person of the opposite sex. In this case have somebody of the same sex lay on hands or let the sick person lay hands on themselves.

7 Persistence

a) Some healing comes not as a result of one or two prayers but over a period of time.

b) It includes:
- regular prayer times
- seeking God for words which will help the situation
- praying into surrounding circumstances or causes
- continuing to show love

8 Different ways in which God heals/ answers prayer

- Instantaneously. If this is so obvious as to need no medical verification, a testimony can help others. Often healing needs to be confirmed medically, particularly as some symptoms come and go.

- Through a process. Keep on praying.

- Spontaneously. Without specific prayer, e.g. during worship and the person finds out afterwards.

- Through medical means.

9 What about those who are not healed?

a) It is important that we never blame them for their lack of faith.

b) Possible reasons for healing not taking place:
- Some people do not believe in healing for today.
- Personal unconfessed sin can create a blockage (although sometimes people can be healed and never even become Christians, e.g. the story of the ten lepers in Luke 17:11–19).
- Persistent and widespread disunity, sin and unbelief in companies of Christians can inhibit healing for individual members (1 Corinthians 11:30).

- Incomplete or incorrect diagnosis, e.g. the root cause is not dealt with.
- General negative attitude to life (hypochondriac).
- Person does not really want to be healed. Jesus asked on one occasion, 'Do you want to get well?' (John 5:6).

c) There is an element of mystery about physical healing. In John 5, even Jesus only healed one out of a large number of people.

- We read about people having long-standing illnesses in the New Testament, even Christian leaders (1 Timothy 5:23; 2 Timothy 4:20).
- There is, for all, a time to die (Ecclesiastes 3:2).
- There are sicknesses which end in death (opposite of John 11:4).
- The reason for this, theologically, is that although the kingdom of God has come, its fullness will not come until Jesus returns, when sickness, sorrow and death will be abolished.
- It is important that we care for the terminally ill and dying. This is an expression of the kingdom just as much as seeing prayer for healing answered.

10 Other miscellaneous points

a) It is important to see what God is doing (John 5:19). However, do not refuse to pray for somebody who comes for healing (although direction of that prayer must be subject to God's leading). There seem to be particular seasons of power for healing (Luke 5:17).

b) Weak points. Many of us seem to have specific parts of our bodies which are vulnerable to stress, tensions, emotional problems and spiritual battles. We may appear to 'lose our healing'. Be aware of this and fight the root causes.

c) It is important that we live healthy lives as well as pray for healing, and make time for the following:

- Regular rest and relaxation. We should try to avoid situations where rest periods make us more tense instead of relaxed!
- Exercise.
- Good eating habits. However, we must not get legalistic.
- Learning how to cope with stress and tension.
- Keeping free of sin, wrong anger, bitterness and resentment, as well as more obvious outward sins.
- Being sociable and friendly.
- Keeping in the love of God and avoiding negative thinking.

Overcoming the Effects of Past Hurts

1 Introduction

● Definition. Healing past hurts is the application in practical terms of what is objectively true in biblical terms. 'Therefore, if anyone is in Christ, he is a new creation; the old has gone, the new has come!'(2 Corinthians 5:17).

Though we are new, we still have to 'put to death' what belongs to the old and 'clothe ourselves' with what belongs to the new (Colossians 3:1–14).

● The purpose. We need to find ways of applying God's truth to the effects of past sins and hurts so that they no longer govern the way we behave now. This does not mean that every painful incident that has happened to us requires prayer.

Our objective is greater freedom in God's service and the extension of God's kingdom, not personal 'wholeness', which will not be attained until glory.

2 Understanding emotions

a) Feelings do matter! It is a false worldview which says feelings are wrong or unimportant. God created emotions. The Bible talks about people weeping (e.g. Jesus at Lazarus' tomb), showing anger (e.g. Jesus in the temple with the money-changers), expressing their depression and anguish (e.g. some Psalms and Lamentations) and showing their love and forgiveness (e.g. the father and his prodigal son).

b) Learn to express rather than deny negative emotions.

c) Emotions are to be brought under the lordship of Christ, e.g. 'In your anger do not sin' (Ephesians 4:26).

d) We are created by God to have a number of sources of emotional health:

   i) A sense of belonging.

   ii) A sense of value derived from being created in the image of God.

   iii) A sense of being able to do things (achievement).

   iv) A sense of felt love.

3 Common emotional bondages

a) Feeling useless

Its origins may be:

i)   Rejection by parents or other significant people.

ii) Lack of approval and praise by parents, schoolteachers, etc.

iii) Pressure to conform to false ideals, e.g. the 'image' of what the ideal man or woman ought to be.

iv) Guilt over a grievous sin.

v) Words that bind, e.g. 'You'll never be any good at that.'

The one talent man in Matthew 25:14–30 presents us with a good example of a sense of unworthiness.

b) Perfectionism

This could also be called 'the bondage of oughts'. Its origins may be:

i)   Rejection, so we react by trying to prove ourselves.

ii) Lack of approval given, e.g. 'You should have done better.'

iii) Inherited perfectionism.

iv) Religious legalism.

Perfectionists usually have real anger underneath, which is often expressed against others who don't conform to the 'oughts'.

Perfectionism can have two possible consequences:

i)   Breakaway. We give up because we find we cannot do anything properly, nor can anyone else.

ii) Breakdown, usually through workaholism.

c) Supersensitivity

Its origins may be:

i)   Rejection. (Satan is a rejected being and rejection rules in his kingdom.)

ii) Trauma.

iii) A lot of shouting or unpredictability in the home.

iv) Violence in the home.

People who are very prickly often set up barriers to stop you getting too close, and may put your acceptance and love to the test before allowing you any closer.

d) Fear

Its origins may be:

i)   Trauma.

ii) Inherited fear.

iii) Occultism and superstition in the family or earlier in life.

iv) Unpredictability in the home.

e) Sexual problems: frigidity or fear of sex

Its origins may be:

i)   Sexual abuse as a child.

ii) Sexual sin in the family tree.

iii) A home background in which sex is regarded as unmentionable.

iv) Other emotional problems as mentioned above.

v)   Promiscuity before marriage or lack of courtship. Promiscuity itself can result from any of the above (i–iv).

f) Sexual problems: homosexuality

Its origins may be:

i)   Inability to form a good relationship with an important male early in life (e.g. father). See the writings of Elizabeth Moberly[1] and Frank Worthen.[2]

ii) A domineering mother.

iii) Sexual abuse as a boy by a man (or another boy).

iv) Rejection in a heterosexual relationship.

Dealing with homosexuality invariably needs more than just ministry sessions.

g) Sexual problems: lesbianism

Its origins may be:

i)   Infantile deprivation.

ii) Possessive and domineering mother.

iii) Estranged femininity.

iv) Fear or hatred of one's father or other men.

v)   Emotional dependency.

h) Rebellion

In one sense we are all rebellious, for rebellion is the essence of sin. However, specific origins may be:

i)   Anger at lack of 'fences' when a child.

ii) Rejection.

iii) Starvation of physical love.

i) Conclusion

Each of these damaged emotions may have accompanying demons, but this is not necessarily so or usually so. There may be shaking, contortions, etc. which are simply expressions of emotion. If we are praying about breaking the power of rejection in someone's life, this does not mean we are expelling a spirit of rejection. However, sometimes the healing prayer brings to light a demon.

Please remember that although we may correctly diagnose the origins of an emotion, that does not excuse us from personal responsibility for that emotion.

4 How do we lead a hurt person to open up?

a) It is essential to show love, acceptance and concern. It may take a long time to build up trust where people have a crushed spirit (Proverbs 15:13; 17:22; 18:14).

b) Watch out for and respond to tell-tale signs, the signals that hurting people send out. Then show particular care. Acceptance will often cause a rejected person to react.

c) Look out for trigger events. Something seemingly insignificant happens that causes a major outburst or deep rejection.

5 Once the person has begun to open up

a) Continue to show acceptance. A rejected person may try to make you reject them.

b) Be open to pictures, words of knowledge, etc. as the person may hide the real reasons for their pain.

c) Sometimes there may be more than one problem.

d) Make sure the ministry to one problem is secure before tackling the next.

e) Allow for expression of pain. In severe cases of abuse, time needs to be taken for 'memory work'.

6 Methodology: values and principles

It is very dangerous to develop a particular model or method. Our work must be based on biblical values and principles, and an openness to the direction of the Holy Spirit.

a) The individual's responsibility

b) Applying biblical truth

For example, we all have value because we are:

● created by God (Psalm 139:13–18)

● chosen by God (Ephesians 1:4)

● loved and redeemed by Him (Galatians 2:20)

● blessed by Him (Ephesians 1:3)

The mind needs to be renewed (Romans 12:2).

c) Forgiveness

What is forgiveness?

i) Taking the offence seriously, acknowledging the pain it has caused.

ii) Letting the other person off the hook, setting your will to never again hold the offence against them.

iii) Walking free of revenge or bitterness.

iv) An act of the will, not of the emotions, deciding to forgive in obedience to Christ because He has forgiven us (Colossians 3:13).

Why is it so important?

i) Healing from past hurts is not intended to excuse us from responsibility for our reaction to hurt.

ii) If we do not forgive we are effectively in prison (Matthew 18:34–35).

iii) If we do not forgive, we harbour hidden anger and resentment.

iv) If we do not forgive, we may fail to acknowledge the other has sinned.

How does forgiveness take place?

i) We receive God's forgiveness for our own sins in the matter, in response to our repentance.

ii) We need to forgive the people who have hurt us, however awful they may have been.

iii) Often there is deep anger against God or against others, which needs to be confessed.

iv) Forgiveness is not cheap.

v) We need to be sure forgiveness has really taken place.

vi) When forgiveness has taken place, healing of the emotions can be received. We need to pray for the person's healing at this point.

d) Cutting the emotional/spiritual umbilical cord

● Very often people have not been emotionally released by their parents.

● People need to be cut off from this in Jesus' name, on the basis of 2 Corinthians 5:17 and Genesis 2:24 (if married), or Mark 3:20–21; 31–34 (if single).

● We must still honour our parents (John 19:26–27).

● Some may have to be led to cut the cord if they are still holding on to their own now grown-up children.

e) Christ as High Priest

Christ Himself suffered and therefore can sympathise with and enter into our sufferings (Hebrews 4:15; 5:7–8). He suffered:

● the stigma of illegitimacy

● rejection by establishment

● rejection by family

● rejection by friends

● rejection by God – so that we may never be rejected!

● lies about Himself

It is often helpful to apply these truths to a hurting person.

f) Other techniques used by some in this ministry

i) Visualisation
    There are a number of objections to this procedure:

- We cannot change history.
- Visualisations can lead to a distorted mental picture of Christ and His character.
- It could involve manipulation, which can become occultic.
- It can result in avoidance of responsibility for our reactions.

ii) The causing of feelings to be expressed.

iii) Beware of mysticism, i.e. any problem that separates mystical experiences from real life.

g) Aftercare

- Continued fellowship, care and friendship is essential.
- The person needs to be taught how to stand firm on the progress made.
- The person must learn to forgive others immediately.

[1] Elizabeth Moberly, *Homosexuality, A New Christian Ethic*, James Clarke & Co 1983.
[2] Frank Worthen, *Steps Out of Homosexuality*, Love in Action 1985.

Healing the Demonised

1 Biblical background

a) Demons exist: they are evil, malevolent spirits with personality. They are under the direction of Satan and can inhabit people and places.

b) A number of expressions are used in Scripture to describe the effect of demons on people's lives:

- Being demonised. This means being affected by or under the influence of a demon to a greater or lesser extent. Scriptures include Matthew 4:24; 8:16, 28, 33; 9:32; 12:22; 15:22; Mark 1:32; 5:5, 16, 18; Luke 8:36; John 10:21.

- Having demons (Luke 8:27)
  a dumb spirit (Mark 9:17)
  unclean spirits (Mark 1:23; 5:2; 7:25; Acts 8:7)
  a spirit of an unclean demon (Luke 4:33)
  a spirit of infirmity (Luke 13:11)

- Being troubled by spirits (Luke 6:18).

- Being afflicted by spirits (Acts 5:16).

- Having seizures (Luke 9:39).

- Being entered into (Luke 8:30; 22:3; John 13:27).

- Being filled (by Satan) (Acts 5:3 – same word as filled by the Holy Spirit).

Nowhere is the word 'possessed' used in the original Greek. This word tends to be frightening and suggests total control or ownership. It is commonly used in translations for 'demonised'. It is preferable not to use it, but to speak of severe or mild demonisation instead.

c) I believe a Christian can be demonised and can be set free. I believe this for the following reasons:

- Scripture describes the phenomenon of demons being cast out or evidently coming out (Acts 8:7).

- If such demons have not been cast out, how have they gone? Scripture gives no warrant for demons automatically disappearing.

- People of faith and those who had previously been filled by the Spirit were, or became, demonised, e.g. the woman with the curved spine (Luke 13:11).

- There are references to our giving a foothold to the devil if we hold on to anger or do not forgive, e.g. Ephesians 4:27; Matthew 18:34–35.

- The story of the Canaanite woman (Matthew 15:26). Deliverance was 'the children's bread', i.e. staple food for God's children.

d) Demons are at work in various ways:

- To tempt us (though not all temptation is demon-induced).

- To oppose/attack us.

- Through demonisation. Demons get a grip to a greater or lesser extent on people's personalities or physical bodies, producing bondages, and patterns of temptation and weakness that are not changed by repentance.

We can all be affected by the first two and need to resist the devil. With demonisation, the demons need to be cast out.

e) We need to be careful about our language. What do we mean by 'a spirit of...'?

2 How do people become demonised?

Common entry points are:

a) Sin. Saul's rebellion (described as being the sin of witchcraft, see 1 Samuel 15:23) led to him having an evil spirit (1 Samuel 16:14). Note the symptoms of this are: fits of anger, murder, fear, witchcraft and suicide. Other sins which often give access to evil spirits include: unrighteous anger, self-hatred, hatred of others, revenge, unforgiveness, pornography, sexual wrongdoing, perversions and abortions.

b) Occult involvement and Eastern religions.

c) Traumatic experiences, i.e. sins against us.

d) Curses or witchcraft against somebody. A lot of this may simply relate to demonic attack (see Proverbs 26:2).

3 Symptoms of demonisation

Often people who claim they are demonised are not! The presence of one or more of the following symptoms indicates the possibility that the person is demonised.

● Unpleasant contorted physical reactions, especially when the power of the Holy Spirit is present.

● Addiction to drugs or alcohol.

● A problem with compulsions.

● A bondage to emotions such as fear, depression, anxiety and rage.

● A bondage to sinful attitudes like self-hatred, unforgiveness, bitterness and resentment.

● Sometimes chronic physical sickness, especially sicknesses that have been in the family for several generations.

● A history of occult involvement.

● A disturbed family history involving, for example, incest, alcoholism and various forms of child abuse.

- Symptoms of rejection (could be emotional only, could be demonic):

    an inability to feel love

    a mistrust of people

    an inability to form lasting relationships

    a persecution complex

    irrational frustrations and anger

    an inability to receive correction

- Symptoms of self-rejection (again could be emotional only):

    deep lack of sense of value

    negative about everything concerning oneself

    lack of self-care

    thoughts of suicide

    NB: The following often run together:

    rejection

    self-rejection

    fear of rejection

    rejecting of others

- Exceptional parental dominance.

- 'Soul ties.' These arise from a very close relationship with an emotionally disturbed or demonised person, or a wrong sexual relationship.

- 'Religious spirits.' People who have been brought up in a very legalistic or superstitious religious system – even if it is Christian – can be in bondage to these spirits (see 1 Timothy 4:1–5).

4 Preparation for ministry

The following preparation is helpful:

- Worship – on our own and with the team.

- Prayer. Have a good prayer base. When Jesus said, 'This kind can come out only by prayer' (Mark 9:29), He was referring primarily to the disciples' general prayer life. Nevertheless, special seasons of prayer and supporting prayer groups may be necessary in difficult situations.

- Always pray in a team of at least two.
- Remind yourself of your own authority in Christ (Revelation 12:11). We are commissioned by Christ to set people free.
- Seek God for the gift of discernment of spirits and words of knowledge. Seek Him for discernment to know when the demon has gone.
- Seek to be filled again with the Holy Spirit and confess and receive forgiveness for any sin in your own life.
- Fix the time of ministry yourself if at all possible. Don't let the demonised person call the shots.
- Try to be private and in a quiet, relatively soundproof place!

5 The deliverance procedure

- Be sure you are working together as a team, with one taking the lead. In severe cases, it is advisable to have somebody experienced and with pastoral authority involved.
- Put the person at ease and take any mystery out of the situation. Explain the truth from Scripture. It is important to ascertain whether the person really wants to be free.
- Pray, inviting the Holy Spirit to come.
- The person you are ministering to needs to repent of sin and renounce evil, forgiving any against whom there is resentment and renouncing any specific occult involvement, whether their own or that of their family. This includes agreement to burn books or occult objects (Acts 19:19).
- Release the person in Jesus' name from curses and family control, if appropriate.

- Command the spirit(s) to go in Jesus' name. You need to be full of truth. Use the name of Jesus and all that signifies (Philippians 2:6–11). Refer to the power of the blood of Jesus, the victory of Jesus over Satan, the power of the Holy Spirit, the empty cross, the empty tomb, the present position of Jesus, the fact that the person is a new creation in Christ and their body is a temple of the Holy Spirit.

- Don't raise the emotional temperature. If it takes time, calm things down, chat with the person and see if there are any footholds yet to be dealt with.

- Pray with eyes open and listen to the Holy Spirit. Ask the person whether they feel the demon has gone, but be careful. If you are not easy in your spirit, the demon may be hiding. Command it to reveal itself to you and then to go.

- If a demon manifests in a particular part of the body it may be helpful to put your hands there (only if appropriate) and/or dedicate that area of the body to the Lord.

- Keep control of the person's eyes if you can, by maintaining eye contact.

- 'Naming' of spirits is a controversial area. The Bible does name certain spirits – e.g. lying spirit, deaf and dumb spirit, spirit of fear, unclean spirit – but whether it is really their 'name' or simply an identification of what they are particularly doing to the person is unclear. I have found that in practice to show that you have uncovered what the spirit is doing can be helpful in causing it to manifest and go. Remember the word 'occult' means 'hidden'. It is also very helpful to the person concerned to help them combat in the future feelings that were caused by the spirit, e.g. rejection, rebellion, etc. However, evil spirits still have to go in the name of Jesus whether we know their 'name' or not.

- Distinguish between manifestations of ejection and manifestations for 'show'. If the latter occur, tell the demon to stop.

- Encourage the person you are praying with to command the demon to go as well.

● If you really don't get through, pray for the person and fix another time, perhaps having prayed further or sought advice.

6 Aftercare

a) Aftercare is very, very important, especially in cases of severe demonisation. The person should be encouraged in:
   ● worship
   ● fellowship with others
   ● building up in the word, particularly scriptures relevant to their situation

b) Demons do try to get back (Luke 11:24, 26). They can regain entry if:
   ● the person persists in sin
   ● they allow bitterness and unforgiveness to come in once more
   ● they are not in close Christian fellowship

c) Walking free. This is as important as deliverance.

7 Backlash

We must not fear it. Resist the devil (James 4:7). Seek prayer cover from others. Persist in your work against the devil's territory.

Practical Implementation

1 Introduction

There are two main contexts in which we are likely to engage in prayer ministry:

● during services

● in prayer teams to 'soak' a situation in prayer

People have different callings:

● some are called to general care

● others will pray for the sick from time to time

● others will have this as a main function in the church

It is important that those who are regularly involved in praying for others in this way have attended an appropriate course and have been released to minister by spiritual authority within the church.

2 Prayer ministry during and after services

Only in extreme circumstances should it be necessary to go out during a service for ministry. Let the person stay in the presence of God.

It is important that prayer should be available for one another in our gatherings, even though there may not be specific ministry times.

The guidelines given at the Stoneleigh Bible Weeks are helpful for public ministry (see appendix).

3 Ministry teams

a) General principles
i)   Accountability and oversight.

ii) Leadership.

iii) Goals and reviews.

b) A few practical hints
i)   Make use of note-taking.

ii) Find a quiet place for ministry.

iii) It is good for the team to meet to pray together prior to counselling.

iv) Encourage the person to develop social relationships. This avoids too much 'navel-gazing'.

v)   Develop relationships with other agencies, e.g. doctors, social services. Sometimes such agencies will talk to a 'minister' in a professional capacity. This can often be very helpful. The permission of the person being counselled is required.

4 Dangers in this ministry

a) The person who 'clings'
Many people fear their lives being overwhelmed by particular needy people. We need to distinguish between:

i)   a problem person

ii) a person with severe problems

What are the differences?

i)   A problem person:
- does not really want to be different
- rarely puts into practice anything suggested but comes back next time with a different problem
- often goes around to different people with different stories (or from church to church)

- has a basic need of repentance
- at first will be very accusatory of others whom they allege have not helped them

ii) A person with severe problems:
- is grateful for the time you spend with them
- will try to put advice into practice
- will be loyal

Sometimes it is difficult to tell the difference at first. In both cases firmness and compassion are needed.

More generally, the following are important:

- Always preserve times of privacy.
- Try to fix times for ministry when it is convenient to you, but recognise genuine emergencies.
- People with real difficulties need to develop general friendships within the church as well as with those helping them.
- This ministry is sometimes a bit risky, e.g. threatened suicides.
- We always need to examine our motives.

b) Emotional dependency

i) Those we are counselling can develop an emotional dependency on us. Talk it through with somebody with pastoral responsibility. Be careful you don't fall for flattery.

Jealousies can emerge and you may feel you are being restricted from befriending others. Don't be bound.

ii) We can become emotionally dependent ourselves. We get so wrapped up in the other person's need that if they fail to respond, we are hurt. Our security must be in God. Leave the results to God.

Particularly be alert to such dependency across the sexes.

c) Manipulation

There can be manipulation:

i) Of you.

ii) By you. For example:

- Controlling someone with guilt so they feel they need to take steps which they are not ready or really willing to take.
- Manipulating someone to freedom which will not bear fruit.
- A wrong use of authority which constantly reminds the individual of your position and their rebellion.

d) Ministry replacing friendship

Our relationship with needy people becomes problem-oriented.

e) Not every problem in people's lives is solved by counselling and prayer ministry

Often what is required is obedience, repentance and a knowledge of truth.

Beware the following:

- Blaming every quirk of character on things that happened in our childhood.
- Avoiding responsibility for sins.
- Constant amateur psychoanalysis of ourselves and others.

f) Ministering out of our own needs

- Nosiness.
- To gain acceptance.
- Feeling self-satisfied when we find somebody else has a problem like ours!

5 The cost of this ministry

- It is costly to minister in this way (see 2 Samuel 24:24).

- It is important to carry on even when things get tough in your own circumstances.

- Beware of counter-attack.

- To engage in ministry you must be prepared to receive it where appropriate.

- It is worth it!

Guidelines for Ministry Teams

Practical matters

- Always submit to your own church team leader, or to any elder or other team leader who directs you.

- Each meeting you will be allocated to a particular block. Seats will be reserved for you at the front of the block with one or two exceptions. You should check with your team leader on arrival in case there are specific instructions concerning that particular meeting. He will have just attended a briefing meeting.

- If for any reason you cannot attend the meeting or intend to swap with another team member (if your church is operating a rota system), then please ensure your team leader is aware of the change.

- Only those with 'Ministry Team' badges will be allowed to pray with people, so *please ensure you wear your badge at all times during ministry*. (NB Please carry your badge with you when not 'on duty' in case you are called upon to help.) Particularly, be available to minister at seminars if required. Please *wear your badge high up* where it can be easily seen by those overseeing ministry – it is not easy to see when it is at the bottom of your jeans or jumper!

- Where relevant, directions for ministry times will be given from the platform. On most occasions, you will pray for people in the aisles. Ensure that there is sufficient room for ministry and don't remove chairs to create space (fire regulations).

Ministering to others

Respecting the individual and helping them feel comfortable

- Before praying, just ask for their name. Later, it may be helpful to ask what is happening.

- Remember personal hygiene. People won't be blessed if you've got BO or have just eaten garlic! Try sucking mints before a ministry time.

- Women on the ministry team must be discreet about what they wear.

- If the person has fallen and they are of a different sex to you, do not bend over them. Let a person of the same sex do that if necessary.

- Avoid counselling. This should be done in a local church context. If you feel that someone needs specialist help during the Bible Week, mention this to your team leader.

- Avoid 'heaviness' or 'intensity'.

- Always retain the dignity of the individual, including confidentiality (though you must feel free to call in your team leader if what is shared with you is 'out of your depth').

- The person you are praying with needs to be assured that they are the most important person at that moment, so don't let your mind and eyes wander onto other situations in the room.

Praying for people to be baptised in the Holy Spirit

- As God moves in His Spirit in various other ways, we must not neglect this essential foundational truth: we believe there could well be people who experience a touch of the Holy Spirit without necessarily receiving the baptism in the Holy Spirit and the power, assurance of God's love and ability to move in spiritual gifts that baptism in the Holy Spirit brings. Please follow the guidelines given to you by your ministry team leader prior to Stoneleigh.

When God moves sovereignly

Let Him do so without getting involved, unless a disturbance is being caused or a person is particularly distressed. Even then, be careful not to 'comfort' if what is actually happening is conviction of sin intended to lead to repentance.

Sensitivity to the Holy Spirit

- Remember what the Spirit has been saying through the ministry of the word and keep focused on Christ.

- Watch what the Holy Spirit is doing. If nothing appears to be happening, speak loving words, encourage them to 'soak' and move on. You could return later.

- Don't pressure yourself or the one you are praying for. Watch the amount of your words, relax and let the Holy Spirit do His work.

- Don't be too subjective but do share the scriptures God brings to mind. If you have a prophetic word (particularly of a directive nature), involve your team leader so that it can be weighed. Be clear when giving the word that the person is free not to take it on board if it does not strike a chord with them. Encourage them to share it with their elder for weighing.

- If people go down in the Spirit, continue to pray for them, inviting the Holy Spirit to continue ministering to them. Be careful not to interrupt when you discern there is a special 'conversation' going on between the person and the Lord.

Prayer engagement

- Pray in pairs, ensuring someone is available to 'catch'. (On the rare occasion you find yourself having to pray for someone alone, only pray with the same sex.)

- The person catching need not necessarily be a member of the ministry team if there are so many people requiring prayer that others are asked to catch. However, non-badged people should not be allowed to get further involved in the prayer ministry.

- If the person has fallen and they are of a different sex, do not bend down over them; let a person of the same sex do that if necessary. The same applies to giving comfort, e.g. putting an arm around someone if they are distressed.

- If you feel unable to deal with a situation (e.g. deliverance), don't press on regardless. Seek help from your ministry team leader. He will have access to those who can minister in specialist areas, if necessary.

- If your hand or body begins shaking, pray with your hands slightly away from the person so as not to distract them.

- If you're a 'catcher', put your hands lightly in the small of the person's back to give confidence.

PERSONAL NOTES